WHY SPACEX IS PARTNERING WITH THE U.S. MILITARY
Race Against Gravity

Story Behind the Rocket Cargo Revolution Poised to Change the Future of Humanitarian Aid

Scott W. Diego

Copyright © Scott W. Diego, 2024.

All rights reserved. No part of this publication may be reproduced, distributed, or transmitted in any form or by any means, including photocopying, recording, or other electronic or mechanical methods, without the prior written permission of the publisher, except in the case of brief quotations embodied in critical reviews and certain other noncommercial uses permitted by copyright law.

Table of Contents

Introduction...3
Chapter 1: The Genesis of the Rocket Cargo Program..7
Chapter 2: SpaceX's Starship – The Key to a New Kind of Cargo Transport................................... 14
Chapter 3: Testing the Limits – Rocket Cargo's Engineering Challenges..................................22
Chapter 4: The Ambitions and Potential Impact of Rocket Cargo.. 30
Chapter 5: AFRL and SpaceX – A Collaborative Journey..39
Chapter 6: Starship's Testing Grounds and Global Logistics Vision.. 47
Chapter 7: Challenges of Adapting Space Technology for Earth-Based Operations..................56
Chapter 8: The Broader Implications of Rocket Cargo on Global Security and Aid........................... 65
Chapter 9: The Future of Space-Based Logistics... 75
Conclusion.. 86

Introduction

In recent years, the synergy between space exploration and military operations has carved out an unexpected path forward. Once, the notion of private companies working closely with the military seemed limited to conventional means of transport, infrastructure, and communications. Yet today, companies like SpaceX have emerged not only as partners in space exploration but as integral forces in reimagining the ways goods, aid, and critical supplies move across the globe. This partnership between SpaceX and the U.S. military, built around the visionary Rocket Cargo program, hints at the dawn of a logistical revolution. With SpaceX's rapid innovations in reusable rockets and point-to-point space travel, the lines between terrestrial and space-bound logistics are beginning to blur.

SpaceX, initially founded to push the boundaries of space travel, has taken an unexpected role in modern logistics. Through this collaboration, the U.S. military is exploring how heavy-lift rockets like

Starship can achieve rapid global reach that surpasses traditional air cargo and military transport. The mission isn't just about speed; it's about rethinking how quickly and efficiently vital resources can reach remote or inaccessible locations in times of crisis. As a private company at the cutting edge of aerospace technology, SpaceX brings to the table a degree of innovation and adaptability that complements the military's strategic needs. Their collaboration raises a compelling question: could this alliance fundamentally alter how humanitarian aid and military cargo are delivered worldwide?

At the core of this partnership lies the shared ambition to change the way logistics work on a global scale. No longer restricted by the limitations of traditional aircraft or shipping routes, the Rocket Cargo program introduces a concept where rockets lift off from one location, only to land on the other side of the world in under an hour. If successful, this endeavor could redefine how quickly aid reaches disaster zones or how swiftly critical military supplies arrive in volatile areas. But the journey is not without challenges. Designing a rocket capable of carrying heavy loads while enduring the rigors of Earth re-entry, or addressing concerns about the environmental impact of repeated launches, demands groundbreaking solutions.

As this partnership between SpaceX and the U.S. military unfolds, it brings a curiosity that reaches beyond logistics enthusiasts. There's something captivating about witnessing a private space company and the military join forces in this ambitious venture. How might such technology impact everyday logistics? Could the same rockets that carry supplies across continents one day bring commercial packages to consumers in record time? This book seeks to dive into the essence of this groundbreaking partnership, exploring the milestones, challenges, and implications of Rocket Cargo. We embark on this journey to uncover not only the technical and logistical breakthroughs that make this vision possible but also the potential for an entirely new approach to moving vital resources, fundamentally reshaping how we think about space, security, and humanitarian aid.

Chapter 1: The Genesis of the Rocket Cargo Program

Military logistics has always been a field driven by necessity, operating under the constraints of time, geography, and complex supply chains. Traditional military cargo transport, long dominated by air and sea freight, has enabled the movement of essential supplies, equipment, and personnel across vast distances. Massive cargo planes like the C-17 Globemaster and C-130 Hercules have historically been the workhorses of military logistics, built to handle large payloads and land on short, rugged runways. These aircraft, along with naval vessels, have been the backbone of military and humanitarian supply chains, used extensively to transport everything from medical supplies to food and shelter in conflict zones, disaster areas, and remote outposts.

However, even with their impressive capabilities, these methods face significant limitations. Aircraft, while relatively fast, can take hours or even days to reach some locations, especially when faced with geopolitical barriers, weather conditions, or terrain obstacles. Cargo ships, while able to carry larger quantities, are even slower, often taking weeks to cross oceans and reach their destinations. In crisis situations, this lag time can have profound consequences. For instance, during natural disasters or sudden outbreaks of violence, hours can mean the difference between life and death for those in need of immediate assistance. The logistics teams must navigate these hurdles while coordinating with local authorities, securing landing rights, and ensuring the safety of both the cargo and personnel involved.

Another inherent challenge with traditional military logistics is accessibility. Remote or landlocked regions can be exceptionally difficult to reach, especially when existing infrastructure has been compromised. While helicopters offer a solution for last-mile delivery in these instances, their limited capacity and range mean that supplies still need to be moved closer to affected areas by larger vehicles first, adding another layer of complexity and delay. Additionally, the operational costs for air and sea cargo transport, especially in emergency scenarios, are substantial. Fuel consumption, maintenance, and crew requirements make rapid-response missions not only logistically demanding but also financially intensive.

These limitations underscore the need for a faster, more adaptable solution to global logistics. In a world where the next crisis could be around the corner, the ability to bypass traditional barriers and deliver critical supplies within hours instead of days is increasingly essential. It's this gap that SpaceX's collaboration with the U.S. military aims to bridge, offering the potential for a revolutionary shift in how aid and resources are transported across the world. The Rocket Cargo program isn't just an exploration of technology—it represents a strategic pivot toward a more resilient, responsive logistics infrastructure that could redefine military and humanitarian support in the years to come.

In 2021, the Air Force Research Laboratory (AFRL) set its sights on a groundbreaking vision: could rockets become a reliable, rapid-response solution for transporting critical supplies across the globe? The concept, dubbed the Rocket Cargo program, was ambitious. Traditional transport methods, while reliable, couldn't match the speed and flexibility that rockets might offer. With this in mind, AFRL launched the program to explore the feasibility of using heavy-lift rockets for point-to-point logistics, envisioning a future where essential military and humanitarian supplies could reach even the most remote areas in record time.

This novel idea didn't just seek speed; it aimed to create a logistics tool that could bypass natural and man-made barriers alike. Whether facing geographic obstacles, hostile environments, or urgent crises, a rocket-powered logistics system could reshape how and where critical supplies were deployed. To bring this vision to life, AFRL needed a partner who was already pushing the boundaries of rocket technology and reusable spacecraft. Enter SpaceX.

With its Starship rocket already in development, SpaceX was uniquely positioned to meet the goals of the Rocket Cargo program. The Starship's design promised not only the payload capacity needed for significant cargo loads but also the reusability and versatility that could make rocket-based logistics feasible on Earth. In early 2022, AFRL awarded SpaceX a five-year, $102 million contract to join forces on this ambitious project. The contract outlined a partnership where AFRL would gain access to SpaceX's commercial orbital launches and booster landings, collecting critical data to assess how Starship could operate as a global cargo vehicle.

Why Starship? Unlike other rockets, Starship was specifically designed to handle significant cargo loads while being able to land intact after each mission. This reusability is essential, as it promises to lower the costs and environmental impact typically associated with rocket launches. Additionally, SpaceX's track record of innovation and rapid iteration offered AFRL a partner that could adapt to the evolving needs of the program. With an extensive history of pushing technological limits, SpaceX provided AFRL with both the technological foundation and the operational expertise to test whether this bold concept could become a reality.

The partnership's goals were clear: explore Starship's potential to move heavy cargo quickly and safely across long distances and gather data on factors such as payload capacity, environmental impact, and landing precision. This data would help determine whether rocket-based transport could indeed become a viable alternative to traditional logistics methods. If successful, the Rocket Cargo program could usher in a new era of rapid-response logistics, one where time-sensitive cargo could be delivered almost anywhere on Earth in under an hour, transforming the way the military and humanitarian organizations respond to global needs.

Chapter 2: SpaceX's Starship – The Key to a New Kind of Cargo Transport

SpaceX's Starship represents a significant leap in rocket design, built with ambitious goals that reach far beyond Earth's orbit. Designed initially for long-duration missions to Mars and the Moon, Starship is unlike any other rocket. Its design focuses on carrying substantial payloads, providing a reusable and fully integrated system that could handle interplanetary transport—a vision SpaceX founder Elon Musk has been vocal about for years. Starship's structure, therefore, is crafted to withstand the unique challenges of deep-space travel, including atmospheric re-entry, rugged landings, and the ability to sustain large loads. These traits, while essential for missions to Mars, have opened an unexpected avenue of potential for Earth-based logistics.

The heart of Starship's capability lies in its reusability. Traditional rockets are generally single-use; they burn through their fuel and often crash into the ocean or disintegrate upon re-entry. In contrast, Starship is designed to land back on solid ground, intact and ready for its next mission. This reusability is critical not only for reducing the costs associated with space missions but also for enabling frequent, rapid launches. SpaceX envisions a future where Starship can be refueled and prepared for successive flights within hours, not weeks. For Earth-based logistics, this rapid turnaround could redefine supply chain dynamics, enabling quick, repeated cargo deliveries anywhere around the world.

Equipped with powerful engines and a massive payload capacity, Starship is capable of carrying up to 100 tons—enough to support complex cargo missions that would otherwise require multiple aircraft or weeks of planning. Starship's design also incorporates an advanced thermal protection system and landing mechanisms to handle the high-stress environment of re-entry, making it adaptable for landing on diverse surfaces, whether it be the arid landscapes of Mars or a remote site on Earth.

While initially developed to survive the low-gravity conditions of the Moon or Mars, Starship's design has the versatility to be adapted for Earth. The Rocket Cargo program has identified these capabilities as key to establishing Starship as a rapid, global logistics solution. For humanitarian missions, this means that medical supplies, food, and essential equipment could be delivered directly to remote areas—regardless of whether there's an airstrip nearby. For military operations, Starship could ensure that time-sensitive resources reach their destinations without the usual delays caused by geographical or political obstacles.

By repurposing the interplanetary capabilities of Starship for point-to-point travel on Earth, SpaceX and the U.S. military are pushing the boundaries of logistics as we know it. The possibility of launching from one continent and landing in another within an hour is no longer confined to the realm of science fiction. Starship's design, with its focus on durability, reusability, and heavy lifting, has made it the perfect candidate for this bold experiment in Earth-based logistics, hinting at a future where rockets might become an everyday tool in global supply chains.

While Starship's design offers remarkable potential for Earth-based logistics, its adaptation to terrestrial missions faces significant technical challenges. One of the foremost concerns is Starship's thermal protection system, which was engineered with the thin atmospheres of Mars and the Moon in mind. Earth's atmosphere, by contrast, is much denser, and re-entry from orbit subjects any spacecraft to intense friction and heat. For Starship to handle this safely and repeatedly, its heat shield must endure temperatures that could easily compromise the vehicle's structural integrity. Achieving reliable thermal protection is crucial, as even minor flaws could lead to catastrophic failures upon re-entry. SpaceX has already encountered challenges with this system in early tests, underscoring the need for further refinement to meet the demands of high-frequency, Earth-based operations.

Another hurdle is the landing propulsion system. Starship's design includes powerful Raptor engines meant to decelerate the vehicle as it approaches its landing site, ensuring a controlled, upright touchdown. However, this system was initially designed to handle the reduced gravitational forces on Mars and the Moon, where the vehicle's mass and descent velocity require less intense braking. Adapting these engines to operate effectively under Earth's gravity, where the gravitational pull is stronger and descent speeds are higher, is a complex engineering task. The landing sequence needs to be precisely timed to avoid overloading the engines, which would risk either damaging the spacecraft or compromising the landing itself. Additionally, landing on a wide variety of terrains on Earth means that Starship's legs must be capable of adjusting to uneven surfaces, a requirement less pertinent in space but critical for this program.

Cargo capacity also presents challenges, not so much in terms of weight—Starship's engines are capable of lifting considerable payloads—but in configuring and securing the cargo within the vehicle. Earth-based logistics often require a range of items, from delicate medical supplies to robust military equipment, which must be safely transported without risk of damage. The vehicle's interior must be adapted to accommodate different cargo types, ensuring that everything arrives intact despite the intense forces experienced during launch and landing. This adaptability is essential if Starship is to meet the versatile demands of rapid-response logistics on Earth.

To address these technical hurdles, the Rocket Cargo partnership has put a strong emphasis on environmental data collection. Each commercial launch and booster landing provides valuable insights into how Starship performs under real-world conditions, from heat management to fuel efficiency. AFRL and SpaceX have focused on gathering detailed data related to atmospheric re-entry, descent speed, heat tolerance, and landing precision. This data serves as the foundation for adapting Starship's design, informing engineers of any required modifications to enhance safety and efficiency for terrestrial missions. By studying environmental signatures and performance across various conditions, SpaceX and AFRL can better understand the vehicle's limitations and strengths.

The partnership's data-driven approach also allows for continual refinement. Each launch provides new information, allowing engineers to test hypotheses and implement improvements, a process that aligns well with SpaceX's rapid iteration model. This constant learning loop is not only critical to overcoming immediate challenges but also to developing a robust, scalable model for Earth-based rocket logistics. The insights gained through environmental data collection will play a pivotal role in determining whether Starship can transition from its original interplanetary focus to a reliable, Earth-based cargo system, marking a shift in how logistics operate on a global scale.

Chapter 3: Testing the Limits – Rocket Cargo's Engineering Challenges

Starship's journey from concept to operational vehicle has been marked by substantial engineering obstacles, each rooted in the demands of Earth's environment and the ambitious goals of the Rocket Cargo program. One of the biggest hurdles lies in achieving successful Earth re-entry. While Starship was initially built for Mars and the Moon, where atmospheric pressure is minimal, Earth's dense atmosphere presents an entirely different challenge. Upon re-entry, Starship encounters extreme heat and pressure that require highly effective thermal protection and structural integrity. This is particularly complex for a vehicle intended to be reusable, as it must withstand these intense conditions multiple times without compromising performance.

Another engineering challenge is the airdrop capability from orbit—a concept that would allow Starship to release cargo mid-flight before returning to a designated landing site. This capability, while theoretically feasible, presents complex technical questions. For one, releasing cargo from a rocket traveling at high speeds requires precise timing and an intricate release mechanism to ensure that the payload is delivered accurately and safely. The dynamics of an airdrop from space differ significantly from those of traditional aircraft, necessitating solutions that can handle the combined challenges of speed, altitude, and gravitational forces. If mastered, this ability could make Starship an ideal vehicle for rapid-response humanitarian or military missions, where flexibility and pinpoint accuracy are essential.

Starship's heavy-lift capacity is another factor that demands significant engineering innovation. While Starship is capable of lifting large payloads—up to 100 tons—Earth's gravity requires a more powerful launch thrust than what would be needed on Mars or the Moon. To reach orbit and deliver such heavy cargo while retaining enough fuel for a controlled landing, Starship's engines and structural integrity must work in perfect tandem. Balancing payload capacity with fuel efficiency and landing capability is a delicate task, and engineers must make critical adjustments to the rocket's design to optimize performance.

These challenges have not been without setbacks. Starship's development has faced multiple failed landing attempts, each highlighting areas for improvement. During early tests, several Starship prototypes exploded or encountered issues during descent and landing. For instance, some test flights saw Starship descend too quickly, overwhelming its landing propulsion systems, while others suffered from instability during touchdown. These failures, while high-profile, have been invaluable learning experiences for SpaceX engineers. Each setback has provided critical data, helping engineers refine the vehicle's landing propulsion, fuel management, and thermal protection systems.

These early tests exposed Starship's vulnerabilities, from engine calibration issues to heat shield durability, and prompted a cycle of rapid innovation. SpaceX has continually adapted Starship's design in response to these challenges, improving its landing stability, structural resilience, and thermal capacity. This iterative approach aligns closely with the goals of the Rocket Cargo program, allowing AFRL to work alongside SpaceX in refining Starship's capabilities specifically for Earth-based operations.

By learning from these failures and addressing Starship's engineering obstacles head-on, SpaceX has been able to push the boundaries of what reusable rockets can achieve. Each test flight, whether successful or not, has contributed to a more robust, adaptable vehicle, bringing the vision of rapid rocket-based logistics closer to reality. Through this process, SpaceX and AFRL are gradually transforming Starship from an interplanetary vehicle into a groundbreaking tool for global logistics, poised to redefine how critical cargo moves across the planet.

The potential for Starship to deliver cargo rapidly across the globe represents a revolutionary shift in disaster response and military logistics. With its capability to carry 30 to 100 tons of supplies, Starship could bypass the limitations of conventional transport, bringing critical resources directly to remote or hard-to-access areas in a matter of hours. For disaster relief, this would be transformative. In the aftermath of natural disasters like hurricanes, earthquakes, or floods, affected areas often face severe infrastructure damage, cutting off traditional supply routes and complicating aid delivery. Starship's ability to land nearly anywhere with minimal infrastructure requirements could mean that emergency supplies—such as food, water, medical equipment, and shelter materials—arrive at the scene without delay, potentially saving lives during the crucial early hours.

Beyond speed, the sheer payload capacity Starship offers could redefine what's possible in humanitarian aid. Traditional aircraft and cargo planes are limited in both range and capacity, often requiring multiple trips or stops, which adds time and logistical complexity. Starship, with its high-capacity, single-flight delivery potential, could bring large quantities of aid in one go, providing relief organizations with the resources they need to sustain operations for days or even weeks without needing immediate resupply. This capability is especially significant in situations where logistical bottlenecks can slow down or even halt relief efforts. By reducing the need for stopovers and in-between transport, Starship could streamline the entire logistics chain, making aid distribution far more efficient and effective.

For military logistics, Starship offers strategic advantages that go beyond speed and payload. Traditional military supply chains, though reliable, can be slow and often require coordination across multiple points, such as airbases and land vehicles. With Starship, essential supplies, ammunition, medical resources, or even heavy equipment could be dispatched directly to frontline or remote military units, reducing the risk of disruptions and enhancing operational readiness. This capability could transform how militaries plan and execute missions, offering a level of flexibility that would allow for quicker responses to dynamic situations.

Furthermore, the strategic advantage of rocket-based logistics lies in its potential to operate beyond the reach of geopolitical and geographical constraints. Traditional transport often requires permission to cross airspace or faces delays due to diplomatic or regulatory restrictions. In contrast, point-to-point rocket travel could reduce reliance on conventional supply routes, giving military and humanitarian organizations a unique tool to work around barriers that might otherwise delay or impede critical deliveries. This independence from typical logistical constraints would provide a level of agility that traditional methods simply cannot match.

Successful cargo delivery using Starship would thus mark a significant milestone in the evolution of global logistics. Whether supporting disaster relief operations in isolated regions or ensuring military units have the supplies they need in real time, Starship's rapid delivery potential could reshape our approach to crises and conflict. In a world where emergencies can arise at any moment, the ability to deliver large volumes of critical supplies rapidly and directly has the power to make an immediate, tangible impact on both human lives and global security.

Chapter 4: The Ambitions and Potential Impact of Rocket Cargo

Rocket-based transport through SpaceX's Starship could redefine the very concept of humanitarian aid delivery. In crisis situations where every second counts, the ability to transport supplies directly from one location to another across continents within minutes could be nothing short of revolutionary. Traditional aid distribution relies heavily on local infrastructure—roads, airports, and ports—that are often destroyed or severely impaired during natural disasters. Rocket transport sidesteps these limitations by offering a method that isn't reliant on existing infrastructure. Imagine, for instance, a flood-ravaged region suddenly receiving life-saving resources, such as clean water, medical supplies, and temporary shelters, in less than an hour, bypassing what would normally take days. The agility of this system could transform the timeline of aid delivery from a matter of days to mere hours, potentially saving thousands of lives during the most critical phases of disaster response.

This rapid-response capability goes beyond just speed. The payload capacity of Starship allows it to transport a substantial volume of essential supplies in a single mission. Large quantities of food, emergency medicine, temporary shelters, and even portable hospitals could be delivered directly to the point of need. This capability could dramatically reduce logistical costs and complexity for aid organizations, which often have to coordinate complex networks of trucks, helicopters, and planes to distribute supplies effectively. Rocket-based delivery could eliminate many of these steps, simplifying logistics and allowing aid organizations to focus directly on relief efforts. Such a system would be especially valuable for reaching isolated or rural areas where help is often delayed or logistically challenging.

The strategic advantages of this rapid transport extend profoundly into military operations as well.

In the realm of defense, the ability to deliver essential equipment and supplies anywhere on Earth within an hour offers a tactical advantage that could reshape military logistics. Conventional military supply chains rely on established routes and supply hubs, which can be vulnerable to disruptions. With Starship, the military could deploy ammunition, medical resources, and other mission-critical equipment directly to active units without delay, ensuring readiness even in rapidly changing or high-risk environments. This could enable forces to sustain operations in areas that are otherwise logistically difficult to support, enhancing resilience and flexibility in the field.

Moreover, rocket-based logistics provide a unique layer of strategic unpredictability. Traditional military supply chains are often visible, relying on well-known air and sea routes. This visibility can make them vulnerable to adversaries who may attempt to disrupt or intercept supplies. Rocket-based transport, in contrast, bypasses these conventional pathways entirely, reducing potential exposure and providing a degree of operational security. In high-stakes or sensitive situations, where rapid resupply is critical, this capability could serve as a valuable advantage, allowing forces to adapt quickly to dynamic conditions on the ground.

The broader strategic implications of rocket logistics reach into geopolitics as well. Military operations frequently face logistical challenges tied to diplomatic restrictions or regulatory issues, with supplies often needing to pass through multiple countries or obtain special clearances. Rocket transport could provide a workaround, allowing for direct delivery without reliance on intermediate approvals. This independence would grant military forces a level of operational freedom previously unattainable, enabling rapid, direct responses without the delays and complexities of traditional transport methods.

Ultimately, rocket-based transport doesn't just offer speed and capacity; it introduces a new level of flexibility, resilience, and strategic reach for both humanitarian and military applications. As crises, both natural and man-made, continue to evolve, the ability to deliver critical resources with unprecedented speed and precision could become one of the defining logistical advancements of the 21st century. This technology stands poised to transform not only the way we respond to emergencies but also the very foundation of global logistics, making rapid, precise, and reliable delivery an attainable reality.

When comparing Starship's capabilities with those of traditional cargo planes, the difference is striking. Cargo aircraft like the C-17 Globemaster and C-130 Hercules, used widely in military and humanitarian logistics, are renowned for their reliability and range. They can carry tens of tons of supplies and operate on short, rugged airstrips, making them suitable for reaching remote locations. However, even these high-performance aircraft are limited by the fundamental constraints of air travel: flight times of several hours or days to reach distant locations, fuel stops along the way, and the need for accessible landing infrastructure. In disaster-stricken regions where roads, runways, or airports may be compromised, these limitations can create critical delays.

Starship, on the other hand, offers a unique capability that fundamentally redefines these logistics standards. With the potential to travel from one point on Earth to another in under an hour, it bypasses the delays of air traffic, international airspace regulations, and conventional refueling needs. Starship's capacity to launch, reach orbit, and land anywhere with minimal ground infrastructure could eliminate many logistical challenges associated with traditional transport. For example, instead of coordinating multiple aircraft to ferry supplies over long distances and difficult terrain, a single

Starship flight could deliver a substantial payload directly to the affected area.

In terms of payload capacity, Starship is designed to carry up to 100 tons, which aligns closely with the larger end of traditional air cargo capacity but offers a significant advantage in terms of immediacy and scale. Whereas air cargo may require multiple flights and relay points to deliver such a volume to remote areas, Starship's heavy-lift capacity and direct-to-site delivery model eliminate the need for these intermediate steps. This would be invaluable during high-stakes missions, where every hour counts, and large amounts of equipment or supplies must be delivered swiftly.

Another advantage lies in the reusability of Starship. Unlike most single-use rockets, Starship is designed to land and relaunch repeatedly, which could, in theory, reduce the costs associated with each mission. While the initial development and launch expenses are significant, the potential for frequent reuse could make it a more cost-effective option over time, especially for high-priority missions where speed and capacity outweigh the costs associated with traditional aircraft logistics. Furthermore, with advancements in SpaceX's rapid launch and landing technology, Starship could be turned around for successive missions in far less time than it takes to refuel, reconfigure, and redeploy a fleet of cargo planes.

Perhaps the most unique feature of space-based logistics is the strategic flexibility it provides. Conventional air and sea routes are subject to diplomatic permissions, international regulations, and physical barriers. A space-based approach allows for a direct point-to-point route, bypassing airspace and geopolitical restrictions that might otherwise delay transport. In military contexts, this offers an advantage by providing a swift, unanticipated method of supply delivery that cannot be easily intercepted or disrupted. Humanitarian missions, too, could benefit from this freedom, allowing aid to reach conflict zones or politically sensitive regions with less risk of interference.

In sum, while traditional cargo planes remain invaluable for everyday logistics, Starship's speed, payload capacity, and operational flexibility offer a new realm of possibilities. By bridging the gap between space travel and terrestrial logistics, Starship has the potential to create a rapid-response supply chain that operates independently of traditional limitations, bringing relief to disaster zones and strategic advantages to military operations with an unprecedented level of efficiency and immediacy.

Chapter 5: AFRL and SpaceX – A Collaborative Journey

The collaboration between AFRL and SpaceX on the Rocket Cargo program hinges on an ongoing, data-intensive process designed to understand and refine Starship's capabilities for Earth-based logistics. From each launch, SpaceX and AFRL collect extensive data covering the critical phases of flight, including liftoff, orbital travel, atmospheric re-entry, and landing. Each data point provides insights into how Starship performs in real-world conditions, informing necessary adjustments in heat protection, landing propulsion, and payload management. The collected data not only confirms what's feasible today but also helps AFRL and SpaceX pinpoint what needs further innovation to transform the program into a reliable logistical solution.

One of the key areas of focus in these tests is the impact of Earth's atmosphere on Starship's thermal protection system during re-entry. Unlike Mars or the Moon, Earth's dense atmosphere poses unique challenges that require precise data to tackle. SpaceX has developed a data-sharing system with AFRL, allowing both parties to analyze real-time performance metrics and adapt accordingly. This collaboration goes beyond observing the technical performance of the vehicle; it involves AFRL researchers and SpaceX engineers working together to understand the environmental effects of repeated rocket launches and assess the sustainability of such operations over time.

Alongside the technical progress made with SpaceX, AFRL's Rocket Cargo program has also expanded its scope by involving additional companies. Recognizing that the future of rocket-based logistics will benefit from diverse industry expertise, AFRL has opened the door to other aerospace and defense companies, inviting them to bring their own innovations and capabilities into the initiative. This broader industry involvement serves several purposes: it accelerates technological advancements through shared knowledge, increases competition, and mitigates risk by diversifying the program's reliance on a single provider. By involving more players in the program, AFRL aims to create a robust and adaptable logistics network that could leverage multiple types of rockets and technologies for different mission needs.

This collaborative approach also encourages rapid progress and innovation. With multiple companies in the race to meet the program's logistical objectives, there is now an ecosystem of shared data, insights, and technology aimed at making rocket-based cargo transport a practical reality. For instance, companies with expertise in landing technologies, reusability, and cargo compartment design are bringing new ideas to the table, each helping to address specific challenges that a single company might not be able to tackle alone. This diversity also provides AFRL with more options, as different companies may focus on specific aspects of the mission, from heavy-lift rockets to specialized re-entry systems, thereby creating a more comprehensive suite of solutions.

In sum, AFRL and SpaceX's data-sharing efforts mark a foundational step in understanding and optimizing rocket-based logistics. The expansion of the Rocket Cargo program to include other companies enhances the resilience and innovation within the initiative, positioning it as a long-term endeavor that could one day revolutionize the way we think about global logistics. By gathering insights from a variety of experts and testing different approaches, AFRL is laying the groundwork for a future where rockets may play an essential role in rapid, adaptable, and efficient supply chains that meet both humanitarian and military needs.

As the Rocket Cargo program progresses, international partnerships have become a critical component in making the concept of rapid, rocket-based logistics a feasible global tool.

Notably, discussions between U.S. and Australian officials have highlighted Australia's unique potential role as a key player in Starship recovery operations. Given Australia's geographic location and vast open landscapes, the country offers an ideal setting for testing and landing large rockets, a factor that could prove essential to the Rocket Cargo initiative.

The collaboration between the U.S. and Australia on Starship recovery is grounded in strategic benefits for both nations. For the United States, utilizing Australia as a landing and recovery site could facilitate broader testing capabilities, enabling Starship to complete longer-range, point-to-point missions across hemispheres. This would allow SpaceX and AFRL to assess Starship's performance over substantial distances, simulating the kinds of rapid logistics missions envisioned for both military and humanitarian purposes. Such long-haul flights provide a more accurate picture of Starship's endurance and environmental impact, as well as its ability to land reliably after crossing continents.

For Australia, hosting Starship landings presents both an economic opportunity and a chance to bolster its own presence in the global space industry. The arrangement would likely bring investment, technology, and expertise to Australian shores, establishing the country as a critical partner in a groundbreaking international logistics endeavor. Australia's remote, uninhabited areas provide the necessary safety margins for test landings, reducing risks and allowing for safer experimentation. In recent meetings, U.S. and Australian officials have discussed the infrastructure and regulatory adjustments that would be required to facilitate these landings, including any adaptations to U.S. export controls to allow Starship's advanced technology to be tested on Australian soil.

This partnership also signifies a broader trend toward global cooperation in space logistics, with countries combining resources and expertise to tackle challenges that span continents. As the Rocket Cargo program gains traction, these kinds of international collaborations could pave the way for an interconnected logistics network that leverages unique geographic and technological advantages from multiple nations. For the U.S., aligning with Australia offers a secure, strategically located partner, one that shares its interests in advancing aerospace technology and expanding emergency response capabilities. For Australia, joining forces with SpaceX and AFRL positions the country as an integral player in cutting-edge aerospace advancements, potentially opening doors to further collaborations in the future.

Through these international discussions, the Rocket Cargo program is creating a template for how countries might work together to support a new era of rapid-response logistics. With testing sites and landing zones that span the globe, AFRL and SpaceX are building the framework for a versatile, far-reaching system that could one day make same-day delivery of essential supplies an international reality. By leveraging Australia's unique landscape and logistical benefits, this partnership is not only enhancing the Rocket Cargo program but also laying the groundwork for global cooperation in space-based logistics.

Chapter 6: Starship's Testing Grounds and Global Logistics Vision

Texas and Australia have emerged as pivotal locations in testing the viability of Starship as a reusable, high-capacity vehicle for Earth-based logistics. SpaceX's launch facility in Boca Chica, Texas, serves as the starting point for most of Starship's test flights, taking advantage of the area's open landscape and access to the Gulf of Mexico for over-ocean launches. Here, engineers can analyze Starship's ascent, orbital capabilities, and initial descent under relatively controlled conditions. Texas provides SpaceX with both the infrastructure and regulatory flexibility necessary for repeated test flights, allowing rapid iteration on design adjustments based on real-time data.

Australia, meanwhile, has been identified as an ideal recovery site for testing long-range, point-to-point missions. Its vast, sparsely populated areas offer ample room for safe landings without the risks associated with densely populated regions.

Australia's remote landscape gives SpaceX and AFRL the safety margins needed for testing full cargo landings while mitigating risks to people and infrastructure. However, using Australian territory for Starship recoveries is not without its complexities. To proceed, both the U.S. and Australian governments must navigate a set of regulatory and legal challenges, particularly around U.S. export controls. The advanced technology within Starship, much of which is subject to strict export regulations, would need specific permissions for transfer to Australian soil. Negotiations around these issues are ongoing, as both countries work toward agreements that would facilitate seamless cooperation without compromising national security or proprietary technology.

Beyond site-specific tests, SpaceX and AFRL are focused on a larger objective: building a sustainable rocket cargo system that could function reliably across a wide range of global environments. This goal involves more than just technical prowess; it requires an infrastructure that can support regular launches, re-entries, and landings in diverse conditions. To achieve this, SpaceX is investing in a reusable design that minimizes the wear and tear typically seen with traditional rockets, which are often single-use. Starship's reusability is at the heart of this sustainable system, allowing each vehicle to perform multiple missions without costly overhauls. However, for true sustainability, Starship must not only be reusable but also able to withstand the demands of repeated exposure to Earth's atmosphere and diverse landing terrains, from the arid deserts of Australia to other potential recovery sites around the globe.

The logistical considerations for such a system are equally complex. Establishing a global network for rocket-based cargo transport requires reliable landing and support sites, flexible regulatory frameworks, and robust environmental assessments. Each site must be equipped to handle high-intensity landings, manage large payloads, and provide quick turnaround services to prepare the rocket for its next mission. These requirements are pushing SpaceX and AFRL to think beyond traditional logistics, exploring how to integrate rocket-based transport into existing supply chains in a way that enhances sustainability and efficiency.

In building a sustainable Rocket Cargo system, AFRL and SpaceX are not only advancing rocket technology but also pioneering a new model for global logistics. They envision a future where reusable rockets can support an agile, adaptable supply chain capable of responding swiftly to crises and operational needs across the planet. This system would offer unprecedented flexibility, delivering resources to places traditional methods cannot reach in a fraction of the time. By focusing on reusability, durability, and global adaptability, the Rocket Cargo initiative is laying the groundwork for a transport network that could one day redefine rapid-response logistics on an international scale.

Implementing rocket-based logistics on Earth brings both financial and environmental costs that must be carefully evaluated to ensure long-term viability. The financial aspect of the Rocket Cargo program is substantial. Traditional cargo transport—whether by air, sea, or land—has established cost structures that, while significant, are relatively predictable and have been optimized over decades. Rocket-based logistics, however, requires a fundamentally different investment model. Launch costs, rocket maintenance, ground support, and turnaround preparations all contribute to a higher operational expense per mission than traditional methods, particularly in the program's early stages. SpaceX's reusable Starship aims to reduce these costs by avoiding the need to construct a new vehicle for each mission. Nevertheless, each launch still entails substantial costs in fuel, personnel, and maintenance, making affordability a key area of ongoing research and development.

AFRL's partnership with SpaceX emphasizes not just the immediate operational costs but the long-term financial sustainability of rocket logistics. By gathering data on launch and recovery expenses, maintenance requirements, and operational turnover rates, AFRL and SpaceX aim to refine the economic model behind Rocket Cargo. The goal is to achieve a balance where the cost per launch becomes comparable to that of traditional air transport—something that will require continuous improvements in reusability and efficiency. As the technology matures, economies of scale could eventually reduce costs, especially if other aerospace companies join the initiative, driving competition and innovation. However, for now, each launch represents a significant investment, and AFRL is carefully analyzing the financial data to assess whether the potential speed and reach of rocket-based logistics justify the costs compared to existing methods.

Environmental considerations are another critical factor, given the high-impact nature of rocket launches. Traditional cargo transport methods, while impactful in their own right, produce emissions on a scale that is relatively well-understood and subject to ongoing mitigation efforts. Rocket launches, however, release different types of emissions, and each launch has a concentrated environmental footprint due to the intensive fuel combustion required to break free of Earth's gravity. AFRL's involvement includes gathering data on these environmental impacts, examining factors like atmospheric emissions, noise pollution, and the ecological impact of frequent landings at remote sites. The program also considers how launch and recovery operations could affect local environments, particularly in areas like Texas and Australia, where Starship's impact on both land and air quality must be carefully managed.

Through extensive environmental data collection, AFRL hopes to determine if rocket logistics can be aligned with broader sustainability goals. This data will help inform adjustments to Starship's fuel use, launch frequency, and landing site protocols, aiming to reduce the ecological impact of the program. For example, if certain environmental impacts are found to be significant, AFRL and SpaceX may explore alternative fuels or modify launch schedules to minimize disruption. Additionally, by understanding the environmental costs, AFRL can work with regulatory agencies to establish guidelines and practices that promote responsible use of rocket logistics, potentially setting standards for an industry that may one day see broader participation from other companies.

In addressing both financial and environmental costs, AFRL and SpaceX are setting a foundation for the responsible, sustainable use of rocket-based transport. Their findings will be pivotal in determining whether the advantages of rapid, global logistics outweigh these costs and whether rockets can be realistically integrated into the logistical landscape without compromising economic feasibility or environmental integrity. Ultimately, the Rocket Cargo program is as much about pioneering sustainable practices as it is about advancing technology, striving to make this vision for rapid-response logistics both financially viable and environmentally responsible for the future.

Chapter 7: Challenges of Adapting Space Technology for Earth-Based Operations

Adapting Starship for rapid Earth re-entry involves an intricate set of design and safety challenges, as Earth's gravity and atmospheric density exert far more force and heat on returning spacecraft than the thin atmospheres of Mars or the Moon. Unlike traditional rockets, which are often designed for single-use re-entry or lighter landings, Starship must handle the intense conditions of Earth re-entry repeatedly, making safety protocols and landing design paramount. Every component must be engineered not only to survive re-entry but also to ensure that the rocket can land with precision and stability, safeguarding both cargo and surrounding areas.

One of the primary challenges in this adaptation is Starship's landing design. Designed to land vertically using its Raptor engines, Starship requires precise control over descent speeds and trajectory to ensure a smooth, safe touchdown. At the high velocities involved in re-entry, even slight miscalculations can result in catastrophic outcomes. Starship must decelerate rapidly upon re-entering the atmosphere, shifting from freefall to controlled descent while adjusting for wind, speed, and gravitational pull. To support this complex maneuver, SpaceX has focused on developing advanced guidance and control systems that adjust Starship's orientation and speed with precision. These systems are bolstered by a series of backup protocols intended to activate if primary mechanisms encounter issues, adding layers of redundancy to enhance safety during high-stress landings.

Thermal protection is another crucial component of safe re-entry, as Starship's heat shield must withstand the extreme temperatures generated by friction against Earth's dense atmosphere. Unlike the relatively calm conditions of space, Earth re-entry produces intense heat, requiring a robust, reusable heat shield to protect the spacecraft's internal components and cargo. SpaceX has incorporated a tile-based heat shield on Starship's underside, designed to absorb and dissipate heat during descent. However, these heat tiles have posed their own set of challenges, as they must be durable enough to survive multiple launches yet light enough to avoid adding unnecessary weight to the vehicle. SpaceX's early test flights revealed vulnerabilities in these tiles, with some detaching or failing under the strain, prompting the company to reinforce the tiles and refine their placement for optimal heat distribution.

In addition to thermal protection, landing propulsion presents a unique challenge for Starship. As it approaches its landing site, Starship must execute a complex "flip" maneuver, where it shifts from a horizontal descent to a vertical position. This move requires precise timing and propulsion control, relying on SpaceX's powerful Raptor engines to decelerate Starship just before it reaches the ground. Given the high speeds and gravity on Earth, this maneuver is considerably more demanding than landings on lower-gravity planets. SpaceX has faced early setbacks in perfecting this system, with some test flights resulting in hard landings or explosions when propulsion failed to slow the vehicle sufficiently. In response, SpaceX has refined its engine calibration and landing protocols, improving the Raptor engines' thrust control and integrating additional stability mechanisms to increase landing reliability.

To further enhance safety, SpaceX has implemented several improvements in Starship's structural integrity, including reinforced landing legs designed to absorb impact on various terrains. These landing legs must be adaptable to a range of surfaces, from rocky plains to sandy or uneven landscapes, making their flexibility and shock absorption vital for reliable touchdown. By engineering each component with both safety and resilience in mind, SpaceX aims to ensure that

Starship can complete repeated Earth re-entries without compromising cargo or crew.

Ultimately, the success of Starship's Earth-based missions depends on balancing these design elements—heat protection, propulsion control, and landing stability—in a way that meets the rigorous demands of re-entry while maintaining the reusability that defines SpaceX's model. As Starship progresses through testing, each improvement in landing safety and thermal management brings the Rocket Cargo program closer to achieving its vision of rapid, reliable cargo delivery on a global scale. The insights gained from these challenges are not just advancing Starship's design; they are shaping the future of reusable, high-performance space vehicles designed to operate in the toughest environments Earth has to offer.

The development of SpaceX's Starship has been marked by a series of high-profile test failures, each of which has provided invaluable insights into the rocket's capabilities and limitations. Far from discouraging the project, these setbacks have become essential learning tools that shape Starship's evolution and bring SpaceX closer to achieving a reliable, reusable spacecraft. From unexpected explosions to landing mishaps, each failure has exposed critical areas for improvement and reinforced the importance of iteration in SpaceX's approach to innovation.

One of the most instructive failures occurred during early Starship test flights, where the rocket encountered difficulties in the landing phase. In these tests, Starship successfully ascended, completed its flip maneuver, and began its descent, only to struggle with final landing stability. Some tests ended in explosions as the rocket touched down too hard, overwhelmed by issues with landing propulsion control and engine timing. These incidents underscored the delicate balance required for Starship's re-entry and landing procedures. In response, SpaceX has adjusted its Raptor engines' thrust calibration, refining the timing of engine relights to ensure that Starship decelerates properly before landing. Each failed attempt has allowed engineers to make fine-tuned adjustments, increasing Starship's chances of a smooth, controlled touchdown in future flights.

Another critical learning moment came with the failure of Starship's heat shield during re-entry. The shield, composed of specialized tiles designed to withstand intense heat, saw multiple detachment issues during test flights, leaving parts of the rocket's structure exposed to extreme temperatures. These challenges highlighted the need for a more resilient heat shield system, particularly for reusable rockets that must endure repeated atmospheric re-entries. As a result, SpaceX reinforced the adhesive used to secure the tiles, improved the design for better heat distribution, and modified the placement of tiles to reduce detachment risk. These iterative adjustments have steadily enhanced the shield's durability, making it better suited for the high-stress demands of Earth re-entry.

The failures have also underscored the importance of structural stability in Starship's overall design. During test flights, engineers observed weaknesses in specific structural components under the intense forces of launch, re-entry, and landing. In response, SpaceX has reinforced these areas to improve the rocket's resilience, adding additional safeguards and stress-absorbing materials to handle the physical strain. The landing legs, in particular, have been re-engineered for flexibility and strength, allowing Starship to land on varied terrain without risking structural compromise.

SpaceX's approach to failure is integral to its rapid development cycle, where each unsuccessful test is viewed as a stepping stone toward progress. This philosophy not only accelerates the pace of innovation but also allows for incremental improvements that might otherwise take years in traditional aerospace development. By iterating on real-world data from each test, SpaceX has been able to refine Starship's design and operational protocols with remarkable speed, building on each setback to make the rocket safer, more stable, and closer to the standards required for the Rocket Cargo program's mission of rapid Earth-based logistics.

These lessons from Starship's failures go beyond technical adjustments; they reinforce a culture of resilience and adaptability. Each test brings SpaceX one step closer to achieving a rocket capable of reliable, reusable, high-capacity missions, pushing the boundaries of aerospace engineering. Through a relentless cycle of testing, failure, and refinement, SpaceX is not only advancing Starship's capabilities but also setting a new precedent for how space technology is developed and improved upon. These lessons will inform every future mission, shaping the way SpaceX and the Rocket Cargo program tackle the challenges of rapid, global logistics on a scale never before attempted.

Chapter 8: The Broader Implications of Rocket Cargo on Global Security and Aid

The introduction of rapid-response rocket logistics could represent a profound shift in humanitarian aid delivery, revolutionizing how and when essential resources reach people in crisis. In the wake of natural disasters, conflict, or medical emergencies, conventional logistics often face hurdles that delay relief, whether due to damaged infrastructure, difficult terrain, or geographic isolation. With SpaceX's Starship, capable of delivering large payloads directly across the globe in under an hour, these obstacles could be bypassed entirely. Imagine a scenario where a region hit by a massive earthquake receives life-saving medical supplies, clean water, and temporary shelters mere hours after disaster strikes, instead of waiting days or even weeks. This swift response could be the difference between life and death, as aid reaches those in need during the critical window where survival rates are highest.

This capability would reshape the traditional model of international aid, reducing dependence on vulnerable transport networks and allowing relief agencies to reach even the most remote locations without delay. The ability to deliver 30 to 100 tons of aid in a single mission would streamline operations for agencies such as the United Nations, Red Cross, and Doctors Without Borders, who often must coordinate complex logistics networks to move supplies. A rocket-based system could not only increase speed but also provide the volume needed to sustain large-scale operations from the onset. Aid organizations could respond to multiple crises across the globe more efficiently, using rockets to establish a supply chain capable of handling simultaneous emergencies and bridging logistical gaps in regions where transportation infrastructure has been severely impacted or doesn't exist.

The implications for military logistics are equally transformative, providing armed forces with an unprecedented level of flexibility and speed. Traditional military supply lines rely on established bases, airstrips, and sea routes, which can be logistically challenging and susceptible to disruption, especially in hostile environments. Rocket logistics could circumvent these vulnerabilities, allowing for the rapid deployment of critical supplies, ammunition, medical resources, and even small vehicles to frontline units. In dynamic combat scenarios, where conditions change rapidly and unpredictably, the ability to resupply troops within hours could enhance operational readiness and provide tactical advantages, enabling military forces to maintain momentum and effectiveness even in remote or contested areas.

Beyond immediate resupply, rocket-based logistics offers strategic implications for global security. By reducing reliance on conventional supply routes, rocket logistics provides armed forces with a level of independence from political and geographic constraints. Traditional supply chains often depend on permissions to cross international airspace or require access to local infrastructure, which can delay or impede critical missions. With point-to-point rocket delivery, the military could circumvent these diplomatic and logistical barriers, ensuring that essential resources reach their destination without interruption. This flexibility would allow military planners to operate with a level of unpredictability that could enhance strategic positioning and reduce vulnerabilities.

The broader adoption of rocket logistics could also reshape the future of defense operations, paving the way for new forms of rapid-deployment and response strategies. Imagine a global logistics network where rockets could deliver not just supplies but specialized personnel or emergency medical teams, creating a rapid-reaction force capable of responding to crises anywhere on Earth. For peacekeeping and humanitarian missions, this capability would be invaluable, allowing for immediate response to emerging conflicts or health crises. For military operations, it represents an entirely new dimension of logistical agility, giving forces the ability to mobilize or reinforce positions in record time, even in areas previously deemed inaccessible.

In essence, rocket-based logistics could redefine the very concept of rapid-response in both humanitarian and military contexts. For disaster relief, it offers a pathway to faster, more effective aid, changing the standard for international response and potentially saving countless lives. For defense, it introduces a level of logistical sophistication that could transform operational planning, bringing new speed, flexibility, and security to global military efforts. In a world increasingly shaped by unpredictable challenges and urgent needs, the ability to deliver vital resources anywhere, anytime, stands to reshape not only logistics but the foundational structures of aid and defense. This new era of rocket-enabled logistics could be one of the most impactful developments in both humanitarian aid and military operations, setting a new global standard for speed and resilience in the face of crisis.

Rocket Cargo technology, with its ability to deliver essential resources rapidly across borders, has the potential to become a powerful tool in shaping international relations and peacekeeping operations. As nations witness the unprecedented speed and reach of rocket-based logistics, the technology could serve as a diplomatic asset, enhancing cooperative efforts in crisis response and reinforcing global alliances. The ability to provide aid swiftly, regardless of geographic or political obstacles, can make a profound difference in international relations, particularly when humanitarian needs arise in areas that are hard to reach by traditional means. A nation or coalition that can deploy aid within hours becomes not only a first responder but a vital partner in times of crisis, strengthening ties with nations in need and reinforcing goodwill on a global scale.

For peacekeeping and international stability, Rocket Cargo offers a strategic advantage. Rapid-response logistics could support peacekeeping forces by ensuring they are well-supplied in challenging regions, reducing logistical vulnerabilities that can hinder their effectiveness. For instance, if peacekeeping troops encounter supply delays due to local infrastructure issues or geopolitical restrictions, Rocket Cargo could bridge these gaps, delivering equipment, food, medical supplies, or reinforcements directly to the mission site. This capability would not only enhance the resilience of peacekeeping operations but also instill confidence in their ability to respond quickly, thereby reinforcing the authority and trust placed in these missions by the international community.

Rocket Cargo could also encourage stronger multilateral partnerships. Nations involved in or supportive of this technology could collaborate to develop shared protocols, training programs, and operational standards that facilitate rapid, cooperative responses. By jointly investing in rocket-based logistics, allied countries could build a collective capability that serves as a resource during global emergencies, from natural disasters to pandemic relief efforts. Such collaboration would foster mutual reliance and deepen alliances, particularly among countries committed to humanitarian aid, disaster relief, and global security. Additionally, countries with strategic locations, like Australia, could become key partners, offering landing or launch sites that make this logistics network even more globally accessible.

However, as Rocket Cargo strengthens alliances, it may also influence global power dynamics. Nations possessing this capability might be seen as leaders in emergency response and logistical innovation, adding to their diplomatic influence. For developing countries or regions affected by recurrent crises, the ability to receive rapid aid from a trusted international partner could ease diplomatic tensions and build long-term partnerships based on shared interests and goals. Additionally, nations or coalitions with rocket logistics capabilities could assume roles as peacebuilding facilitators, using their unique resources to stabilize regions in conflict through consistent, reliable support.

Yet, the expansion of Rocket Cargo also requires responsible implementation to prevent potential misuse. Ensuring that the technology is used solely for humanitarian aid and defense logistics, rather than as a tool for political leverage, will be critical to its acceptance and sustainability on the global stage. Transparent protocols, international oversight, and cooperation with global organizations such as the United Nations could help Rocket Cargo become a trusted tool for good, supporting international stability without raising concerns of dominance or coercion. Properly managed, Rocket Cargo could become a pillar of international relations, empowering nations to support each other more effectively while fostering peace and resilience.

In this light, Rocket Cargo could transcend its technical and logistical roots, becoming a catalyst for closer global cooperation and a model for how technology can be harnessed to serve shared human needs. Its influence on alliances, peacekeeping, and global crisis response could set a new standard for international partnerships, showing how innovation in logistics can drive diplomacy, build trust, and reinforce a collective commitment to humanitarian support and security. In a world where crises often outpace traditional responses, Rocket Cargo's swift, borderless reach offers a hopeful new vision for international relations in the twenty-first century.

Chapter 9: The Future of Space-Based Logistics

The potential for rocket-based logistics to extend beyond military use opens up an exciting frontier for commercial and civilian applications. While the Rocket Cargo program initially focuses on rapid-response solutions for defense and humanitarian aid, the same principles could one day revolutionize sectors such as e-commerce, medical logistics, and global supply chains. Imagine a world where goods can be delivered internationally within hours rather than days, connecting suppliers, retailers, and consumers with unprecedented speed and efficiency. The high-speed, long-distance delivery enabled by rockets could fundamentally reshape expectations for global commerce, reducing delays and opening new opportunities for businesses that rely on fast, reliable shipping.

One promising application lies in medical logistics. For remote or underserved communities, access to critical medical supplies can be hampered by long transportation times or unreliable infrastructure. Rocket-based logistics could bypass these barriers, enabling hospitals, clinics, and research facilities to receive essential medications, vaccines, and even medical equipment in a fraction of the time traditional shipping allows. In scenarios where timing is critical—such as delivering organs for transplant or urgently needed vaccines during outbreaks—rocket-based transport could be life-saving. Pharmaceutical companies and healthcare providers could use this technology to ensure rapid, consistent delivery to areas that currently face logistical obstacles, helping bridge healthcare gaps and improve access to timely treatment.

E-commerce is another field where rocket-based logistics could create groundbreaking changes. As consumer expectations for quick delivery continue to rise, companies like Amazon, FedEx, and UPS are constantly looking for ways to speed up shipping. With rocket-enabled logistics, cross-continental deliveries could reach customers within hours, creating a new standard of ultra-fast, global delivery. The ability to launch a payload from one continent and have it delivered to the other side of the world within the same day would be a transformative capability for e-commerce giants. Such logistics would enable companies to manage inventory globally, bringing products directly to consumers or distribution centers as needed without relying on extensive warehousing in every market. This approach could reduce storage costs, streamline supply chains, and redefine what's possible in international commerce.

The agricultural industry might also benefit from rocket-based logistics, particularly for transporting perishable goods. Currently, transporting fresh produce across long distances requires carefully managed supply chains to maintain freshness, especially when shipping from one hemisphere to another. Rocket transport could shorten the journey from farm to table, minimizing spoilage and preserving nutritional quality, while expanding market access for farmers and producers in remote regions. This system could open up new trade opportunities and allow consumers around the world to access fresh, high-quality produce year-round, regardless of seasonal or geographic limitations.

For scientific and environmental research, rapid logistics via rocket could enable swift transport of sensitive data samples, rare biological specimens, or field equipment. Scientists working in extreme or isolated environments, like the Arctic or deep ocean research sites, often need specialized equipment or replacement parts that are challenging to ship quickly. Rocket-based logistics could offer a new level of support for these efforts, ensuring that supplies arrive promptly, enabling uninterrupted research, and providing rapid evacuation options for urgent medical situations.

As rocket logistics become more accessible and refined, there's also potential for this technology to support international disaster relief on a commercial basis, enabling private organizations and NGOs to use rapid delivery for targeted relief operations. While initially developed with government and defense applications in mind, a broader infrastructure for rocket-based logistics could eventually allow private entities to use this technology for aid missions, bringing together government, non-profit, and commercial resources to create a globally responsive logistics network for crisis situations.

However, achieving this vision for civilian and commercial use will require significant advancements in cost-efficiency and regulatory adaptation. For rocket-based logistics to be feasible on a large scale, the cost per launch will need to decrease substantially, making it competitive with or complementary to current air cargo rates. Additionally, integrating rockets into civilian airspace and international transport frameworks will require updated regulations, airspace coordination, and environmental considerations to ensure that increased launch frequency does not adversely impact communities or the environment.

Ultimately, the evolution of rocket-based logistics could transform how we think about distance, time, and accessibility in commercial and civilian sectors. As the technology matures and operational costs decrease, we may one day live in a world where rockets are not only symbols of space exploration but also integral tools in our everyday lives, connecting people, resources, and opportunities across the globe at unmatched speed. The transition from military to civilian and commercial use could make rocket logistics one of the most revolutionary developments of the century, reshaping our global economy and bringing the future closer to hand.

As the Rocket Cargo program gains traction, it opens the door for innovation and expansion across the aerospace and logistics industries, inviting more companies to join in and bring fresh ideas to the table. Currently, SpaceX is at the forefront of rocket-based logistics, but as the concept proves viable and demand grows, other aerospace players may enter the field, fostering an environment ripe for innovation and competition. Established companies like Blue Origin, Northrop Grumman, and Sierra Space, each with their own expertise and infrastructure, are likely candidates to join or develop complementary technologies. Such involvement would not only diversify the technological approaches within the Rocket Cargo initiative but also drive advancements at a pace that can only be achieved through competitive, collaborative industry efforts.

A broader industry presence would enhance the Rocket Cargo ecosystem by introducing new technologies, different rocket designs, and logistical solutions. Competition typically accelerates technological improvements, as companies strive to make their rockets more cost-effective, fuel-efficient, and reliable. By involving multiple companies, AFRL's Rocket Cargo program could benefit from varied solutions to the unique challenges of Earth-based rocket logistics, such as landing reliability, fuel efficiency, and environmental sustainability. This diversity would provide AFRL with a range of capabilities suited to different types of missions—lightweight, high-speed cargo delivery, for example, versus heavy-duty shipments. A multi-company landscape would likely create a robust, adaptable system that could meet varied logistical needs, making space-based logistics a versatile addition to global supply chains.

AFRL's long-term vision for the Rocket Cargo initiative is one of sustained growth, gradually transforming rocket logistics from a specialized defense tool into a mainstream industry. By establishing partnerships with SpaceX and other aerospace leaders, AFRL is laying the groundwork for a space-based cargo industry that could operate on a global scale. The agency envisions a future where rockets are a reliable option for Earth-bound logistics, allowing for rapid, on-demand delivery capabilities that transcend the limitations of traditional air and sea transport. AFRL's roadmap includes working toward cost reductions and operational efficiencies, aiming to make rocket logistics viable for civilian, commercial, and humanitarian uses. By collaborating with private companies and promoting industry standards, AFRL hopes to encourage a sustainable industry model that can operate independently of defense needs, transforming rocket-based logistics into a staple of the global economy.

SpaceX's commitment to this vision aligns with its overarching goal of making space accessible and useful for humanity on a daily basis. Starship's development, driven by reusability and high-capacity transport, is at the heart of this long-term vision, with SpaceX aiming to create a fleet of rockets that can operate as frequently and reliably as commercial airliners. Through continual refinement and a rapid iteration process, SpaceX is focused on reducing the costs associated with rocket launches and advancing Starship's capabilities, positioning it as the ideal vehicle for regular, high-speed cargo missions. The company's dedication to transforming logistics reflects its broader mission of democratizing space, providing a scalable solution that could one day support everything from humanitarian aid to global e-commerce.

In the grand scheme, AFRL and SpaceX's collaborative work on Rocket Cargo is setting the stage for a revolutionary new industry. The technology and operational standards established in this early phase will act as a foundation for future participants, creating a playbook for how rocket logistics can integrate with existing global supply chains. As more companies enter the arena and technology continues to advance, rocket-based logistics could transition from experimental to indispensable, a regular feature in the world's response to both routine and urgent logistical challenges. The long-term vision for Rocket Cargo is not just about delivering cargo faster—it's about creating a resilient, adaptive logistics system that brings the benefits of space technology into everyday life, reshaping the landscape of global transport and connectivity for generations to come.

Conclusion

The Rocket Cargo program stands at the threshold of a new era in global logistics, combining advanced aerospace technology with the urgent need for faster, more adaptable supply chains. At its core, Rocket Cargo brings together SpaceX's ambitious Starship capabilities and the U.S. military's vision of rapid-response transport, offering a revolutionary solution to the limitations of traditional air, sea, and land logistics. Through rocket-based delivery, humanitarian aid can reach crisis zones in a fraction of the time, bypassing damaged infrastructure and geographical obstacles. Military operations can rely on a swift, dependable resupply system that supports forces in remote or contested areas with a speed and precision unimaginable before.

The potential applications for Rocket Cargo extend far beyond immediate military and humanitarian needs. The framework being developed today hints at an expansive future where rocket logistics support commercial industries, scientific research, and even agricultural supply chains, making swift, global delivery feasible for a variety of sectors. With the capacity to carry substantial payloads across continents in under an hour, Starship could redefine how industries think about supply timelines and logistics costs, while transforming public expectations for rapid, reliable delivery. The development of such a system has required overcoming challenges, from thermal protection on re-entry to the coordination of global launch and landing sites, and each milestone reached has brought the program closer to proving the feasibility of rocket-based transport.

Looking ahead, the next steps in Rocket Cargo's evolution are critical. Upcoming test flights will provide further data on Starship's performance in high-stress, Earth-based environments, with a focus on refining its reusability, efficiency, and cost structure. International partnerships, such as those with Australia, will play a key role in establishing a global infrastructure for rocket landings and recoveries, setting the foundation for a truly worldwide logistics network. In the near future, the first successful Rocket Cargo missions could provide proof of concept on a large scale, demonstrating that this vision of logistics is not only possible but practical and transformative.

The long-term implications of Rocket Cargo reach beyond logistics, positioning it as a cornerstone of a more interconnected and responsive world. SpaceX and the U.S. military, through AFRL, are pioneering an entirely new logistical framework, one that has the potential to make rapid, cross-continental delivery an everyday reality. This capability could redefine our approach to humanitarian aid, military operations, and commercial transport, enabling resources to move seamlessly across borders and helping to bridge gaps between nations and communities. By bringing space technology down to Earth, Rocket Cargo offers a glimpse into a future where the world is more connected, responsive, and resilient.

In the end, Rocket Cargo's journey is just beginning, but its impact may one day be felt across every corner of the globe. As this technology advances, it holds the promise to reshape our understanding of time and distance, forging a new frontier in logistics that reaches far beyond what we once thought possible.

www.ingramcontent.com/pod-product-compliance
Lightning Source LLC
Chambersburg PA
CBHW070259220526
45465CB00004B/1664